Positively Puppets!

Anita Louise Brezovic Vance

ISBN 978-1-0980-9691-5 (paperback)
ISBN 978-1-0980-9692-2 (digital)

Christian Faith Publishing, Inc.
832 Park Avenue
Meadville, PA 16335
www.christianfaithpublishing.com

Printed in the United States of America

Welcome to *Positively Puppets!*, a collection of short puppet plays designed to help understand New Testament gospel readings. Each play gives the audience a thoughtful discussion in simple, direct language. Originally used as a children's time sermon, it includes pastoral interactions and engages the entire congregation in exploring the message of the week.

Minimum prep, a single puppeteer, and simple props make these plays easily reproducible in various settings such as vacation Bible school, parent-teacher nights, school assemblies, class presentations, etc.

Our original stage was a three-panel room divider where puppets were shown at the top. For puppeteers, this can be a painful angle for performance. A second stage was constructed from a mobile closet storage frame. Twin-sized sheets were just the right size to drape and adjust for framing, and a lower stage opening made performance more comfortable as well. The interior space accommodates a single puppeteer and a microphone.

Fishing for Men
(Matthew 4:18+)

Items needed: two puppets, toy fishing pole tied with mini chocolate bar bait, small stuffed animal toy, and any mouth puppet

(*Buddy enters with a fishing pole, pulls it around with a toy lamb attached.*)

BUDDY. I'm almost finished with my "Fishing for Men" project.

LAMB. Wheeeee! Do it again! Do it again!

BUDDY. Wait! You already had one! Come again tomorrow for some more.

LAMB. Okay! (*Exits.*)

(*Buddy swings the line with a candy bar behind stage. Giraffe [mouth puppet] enters with the chocolate bar in mouth.*)

GIRAFFE: Mmmf! Mmmmm. (*Sees kids.*) Oh my!

BUDDY. Did you like it? Would you like some more?

GIRAFFE. What is it? I am a vegetarian. I won't eat just anything!

BUDDY. Oh, you will like this! It has zero calories. It is a holy blessed bar of chocolate.

GIRAFFE. Mmmm. It's not bad, but it had a hair on it! I don't think I want it anymore. (*Exits.*)

BUDDY. Come back anytime! I have more. Now just one more, and I will have given them all away today. I have been sooo good!

PASTOR. Buddy, what are you doing?

BUDDY. I'm fishing for men, just like it says in today's gospel.

PASTOR. That is today's reading, but I don't see how you—

BUDDY. Oh, it's super easy! You will be so proud of me, and anyone can do it!

PASTOR. I'm almost afraid to ask… Do what, Buddy?

BUDDY. Well, I take my fishing pole, add a holy blessed bar of chocolate, and when someone eats it, they are blessed forever, and I have fished for Jesus.

PASTOR. I've never heard of a holy blessed bar of chocolate. I think I would know about that!

BUDDY. I just invented it! I sprinkled some candy bars with holy water, and now they are holy blessed bars of chocolate!

PASTOR. Hmmmm. I hate to tell you this, Buddy, but it doesn't work that way.

BUDDY. But why not? Sissy says you are what you eat! And Jesus said to go fishing for men!

PASTOR. I know it sounds possible, but you can't know all about Jesus just by eating something. When you are fishing for men, you are telling and showing everyone the message Jesus gave—that God loves all of us, and He wants us to love each other too.

BUDDY. Oooooh! So no fishing pole?

PASTOR. Nope!

BUDDY. Just telling and showing?

PASTOR. Yes.

BUDDY. That's a little harder.

PASTOR. Yes, it is.

BUDDY. But that sounds like Sissy's favorite song!

PASTOR. It does!

BUDDY AND PASTOR. Share a little faith with me, and you'll see how we keep on trying. Add a little prayer and see blest are we! (*Melody: chorus from "Smile a Little Smile for Me, Rosemarie."*)

Transfiguration (Matthew 17:1–9)

Items needed: female puppet, embellished jacket, small wooden crosses for each child

(Sissy enters with an embellished jacket.)

Sissy. Oh, I'm so excited to give this to Buddy—I want to how him how proud I am of all his projects about Jesus. This piece is because he helped Mikey sing, this piece is for helping feed the birds in our yard, and this piece is for fishing for souls. Isn't it marvelous?

Pastor. Hello, Sissy! What is this?

Sissy. I was just telling everyone about this marvelous jacket I embellished for Buddy!

Pastor. Is there a special occasion?

Sissy. No, but the story about Jesus on the mountain, in dazzling white and talking to the prophets, inspired me.

Pastor. Hmm. How did that story lead to this jacket?

Sissy. Well, God was so proud of His Son, Jesus, that He showed Jesus's friends how He really looked in heaven.

Pastor. Yes, go on.

Sissy. And I wanted to show Buddy how proud I am of him as he tries to show everybody how much Jesus loves them!

Pastor. Oh! Now I understand—you are trying to make a dazzling jacket for Buddy.

Sissy. That's it!

Pastor. But, Sissy, do you remember how the story ended?

Sissy. Oh yes! Peter is going to build a church to remember!

Pastor. Well, not exactly—Peter *wanted* to build a church, but Jesus told them all not to speak of it again until Jesus had risen from the dead. Jesus only wore dazzling clothes once, and only for a minute.

Sissy. Well then, how can I show Buddy that he is doing so well? He is working so hard to show everyone how much God and Jesus loves us.

Pastor. When Jesus wanted to show us his heart, he showed us something else. Sometimes the simplest way is the best—I may have something that will work. (*Shows a simple wooden cross.*)

Sissy. Oh! That is perfect! He can wear that or put it in his pocket, and it will always remind him about Jesus! I was wondering how I would ever wash this jacket anyway! Pastor, you are very good at finding a good way for all of us to work together.

Pastor. We are getting better at that—I even have enough simple crosses to share with our children today. (*Distributes the crosses.*)

Sissy. How wonderful and marvelous! I feel like singing! Could you join us?

(*Sissy and Pastor sing to the melody of the chorus of "Smile a Little Smile for Me, Rosemarie" by the Flying Machine.*)

Sissy and Pastor. Share a little faith with me and you'll see, how we keep on trying. Add a little prayer and see, blest are we!

Forgive One Another
(Matthew 18:21–35)

Items needed: Buddy puppet, female puppet, toy vehicle, puppet-sized duster

(*Buddy enters, playing with a toy and exits. Sissy enters, humming and dusting.*)

Sissy. Ouch! Oh, what is that? (*Picks up car.*) Buddy! Come pick up your toys!

Buddy. I did pick them up. I picked up all my Legos.

Sissy. What about the cars?

Buddy. You didn't say anything about them.

Sissy. Buddy, you know I meant all of your toys.

Buddy. That's not what you said!

Sissy. Buddy, you are not being very nice. Look at all our friends. They are surprised at you!

Pastor. Now, Buddy, be nice.

Buddy. I don't wanna be nice—I'm tired of being nice!

Sissy. You've already lost some bedtime privileges. Are you looking for more?

Buddy. I don't care—I never get to do anything anyway!

Sissy. Excuse me? Is that the way you talk to me?

Buddy. No, ma'am. I'm sorry. May I start over? I'll try harder, I promise.

Sissy. Are you really?

Buddy. Yes, ma'am, I'm really sorry. I'll do better, I promise!

Sissy. I don't know. What do you think, Pastor?

PASTOR. Buddy? Are you really ready to start over?

BUDDY. Oh yes! I'm ready to try harder to be better!

PASTOR. Well then, I think we should give him another chance.

BUDDY. Yay! Thank you! I'm going to get all my toys picked up.

(*Buddy reappears with a broken toy.*)

BUDDY. Why don't you work right anymore? I'm tired of fixing you over and over—you are ready for the trash!

(*Squeaker responds. Buddy exits.*)

SISSY. What am I hearing? (*She sees Squeaker.*) Oh no, how did you get in the trash? Buddy put you there because you are broken? Oh, you poor thing? Look, Pastor! (*Shows Pastor.*) This is like the Bible story I just read about the slave who owed his master, but he said, please forgive me, and the master forgave him his debt, but then that slave was mean to his helper.

PASTOR. That's right! See? It just needs to be cleaned up a little—we can help it look good as new in just a minute! There!

BUDDY. Hey, what are you doing with that nasty old thing?

SISSY. That used to be one of your favorites!

PASTOR. It just needed a little help—a chance to clean up and start over.

BUDDY. Oh, I see. Just like me. Thank you for both of us!

SISSY. Oh, I just love happy endings—it makes me feel like singing!

BUDDY AND PASTOR. We know!

(*Everyone sings to the melody of the chorus of "Smile a Little Smile for Me, Rosemarie" by the Flying Machine.*)

SISSY. Share a little faith with me, and you'll see how we keep on trying.

BUDDY. Add a little prayer and see, blest are we!

Talents (Matthew 25:14–30)

Items needed: two puppets, toy jingle, and a toy clapper

(*Buddy enters with the jingle.*)

BUDDY. I'm so excited! Sissy says if we practice, we can share a song with all of you! I'm gonna sing the bird song about the geese! (*Sings off key while jingling.*) When geese on the river can fish with a pole—no, that doesn't sound right. When geese on the river—

PASTOR. Buddy, what are you doing?

BUDDY. I'm practicing my talent. When geese on the river... (*Jingles.*)

PASTOR. Wait. I think you have the words mixed up. It goes like this. When peace like a river attendeth my soul...

BUDDY. It's not about geese? And no fishing? Hmmm. Wait till I tell Sissy how mixed up she is! (*Exits.*)

(*Mikey enters with clapper.*)

MIKEY. Owls can smell, Owls can tell in the snow. Or is it, Owls can tell, Owls can smell in the snow?

PASTOR. Mikey, what are you doing?

MIKEY. Probably nothing. Buddy wanted us to do something for Talent Sunday, but I never get stuff right.

PASTOR. Well, I could help you a little with that. You have the words mixed up. These are the real words. (*Sings.*) It is well, it is well with my soul.

MIKEY. Oh, that does make more sense. See? I can't even get the words right. I'm not sure I want to do anything. (*Exits.*)

(*Buddy enters with jingle.*)

BUDDY. Attendeth my soul, when sparrows like sea biscuits grow...

PASTOR. Buddy, try this. When sorrows like sea billows roll. What is this all about?

BUDDY. Sissy said that if I practiced, I could do something for Talent Sunday.

PASTOR. Talent Sunday?

BUDDY. Yes. The Sunday when the story is about talents that get buried and the servant gets kicked out? I don't want to get kicked out, so I'm practicing my talent. I'm making it better by investing my time.

PASTOR. Oh, I see! I like that you are investing your talents by practicing. Mikey was trying to do something too.

BUDDY. He just told me he's not coming with me. He's not practicing and won't come out. He's very sad, and I'm sad too.

PASTOR. Maybe we can work together to help him. If everyone calls Mikey, maybe he will come out. One, two, three, MIKEY!

(*The top of Mikey's head appears and disappears.*)

PASTOR. Let's try again. One, two, three, MIKEY!

MIKEY. What do you want? I'm not doing anything.

BUDDY. But you wanted to play and sing with me.

MIKEY. I can't do it right. I'm not gonna do it at all!

BUDDY. Yes, you can. You just need to invest in yourself and in your talents so you can shine for Jesus.

MIKEY. Do you really think so?

BUDDY. Yes! C'mon, Mikey. We can do this! I want my best friend to invest his talents too! C'mon, everyone. Sing with us!

(*Everyone sings while the puppets accompany with clapper and jingle.*)

POSITIVELY PUPPETS!

When Peace like a river attendeth my soul,
when sorrows like sea billows roll.
Whatever my lot, thou hast taught me to say,
it is well, it is well with my soul.
It is well, with my soul,
It is well, it is well with my soul.

(*Puppets bow and exit.*)

Tricksters (Matthew 22:17+)

Items needed: three puppets—one large, one small, and one female puppet, dollar bill on a black wire

(*A dollar bill floats into view and lands on the middle of the stage. Buddy excitedly runs in and reaches for it.*)

BUDDY. Woohoo! My lucky day!

(*Just as he reaches down, Mikey Mouse pops up and takes it.*)

BUDDY. Hey! You can't have that. It's mine!
MIKEY. No, it's not—it landed right at my door. It's mine!
BUDDY. It came off my money tree. It's mine!
MIKEY. You have a money tree? Then you won't mind if I have it 'cause you have more.
BUDDY. No, it takes a long time to grow a dollar bill. I have been waiting for two days since I buried my penny.
MIKEY. You can't grow money. You are trying to trick me.
BUDDY. No, I'm not. I buried a penny, and a dollar appeared in two days—that dollar right there. Hmmm. Maybe we should bury my dollar by my penny.
MIKEY. And more dollars will grow! We should bury it right here by my door, and I could watch it, and I could tell you when there is another.
BUDDY. Hey, are you trying to trick me? Give me back my dollar!
MIKEY. It's not your dollar, I grabbed it first. (*A scuffle ensues.*)
PASTOR. Boys, stop fighting! Boys—

(*Sissy enters.*)

SISSY. What is all this about? Boys? Boys? Boys!

(*Both boys stop and look up.*)

BUDDY. He has my money!
MIKEY. He has my money!
SISSY. Oh? How do either of you have *any* money?
BUDDY. I grew it in the garden.
MIKEY. It landed in my doorway.
SISSY. Sooo it doesn't really belong to either of you.
BUDDY. But, but, but... I grew it!
MIKEY. But, but, but... I found it! Finders keepers.
SISSY. Verrry interesting. But neither of you earned it or worked for
    it.
BUDDY. I planted it, and—
MIKEY. No—
SISSY. Pastor, isn't this interesting? First of all, Buddy, you know you
    can't just plant anything. Remember the M&Ms and the lolli-
    pops? Did they grow anything?
MIKEY. You planted M&Ms? Too bad they didn't grow.
BUDDY. They didn't grow 'cause they weren't real seeds. Ooooh! I
    guess a penny isn't a real seed either.
SISSY. But we do have this dollar that you found.
PASTOR. How will we figure this out?
BUDDY. I know. I can describe it—that will prove that I own it just
    like lost and found.
MIKEY. So can I—it's rectangular and green, so I claim it.
PASTOR. Hey, now you are trying to trick me!
SISSY. Hmmmmm. Is there anything written on it?
PASTOR. Yes, there is. It says, "In God we trust"
MIKEY. Ohhh! Buddy, it's God's!
SISSY. Maybe in this case, it is! Did you work for or earn this dollar?
    People use money in payment for work, or to pay bills, or pay
    taxes, or buy things they need. You don't do any of that. Maybe

15

instead of tricking each other, you could donate it where it will do God's work. Remember Jesus told his tricksters to "give to God the things that are God's."

BUDDY. Pastor, could we donate this to help hurricane victims?

MIKEY. Yes, that will be for God's work.

PASTOR. Why yes, what a good idea! I'm proud of you for thinking of that.

SISSY. I am too! Another happy ending! I feel like singing!

(*Everyone sings to the melody of the chorus of "Smile a Little Smile for Me, Rosemarie" by the Flying Machine.*)

SISSY. Share a little faith with me, and you'll see how we keep on trying.

MIKEY. Add a little prayer and see.

BUDDY. Blest are we!

Keys to the Kingdom
(Mark 17:19)

Items needed: two puppets, lock, keys

(*A lock is visible from the front of the stage.*)

BUDDY, *thumping and sobbing.*

PASTOR. What is this? What is happening?

BUDDY. Is anyone there? Can you hear me?

PASTOR. Buddy? Is that you? What happened?

BUDDY. I'm stuck in here! I wasn't supposed to play here, but I tried to get Bobo, and now I'm stuck.

PASTOR. What? What is a Bobo? How are you stuck?

BUDDY. Bobo sleeps with me. He keeps me safe. I dropped him while we were playing. I know I wasn't supposed to play here, and now I'm stuck. It's locked, and no one can help me.

PASTOR. Where is the key? We can help you.

BUDDY. I did something bad, I let down my friend. No one has the key, and now I'm stuck forever. (*Crying loudly.*) I want my Sissy!

SISSY. What is all this noise? (*Sees lock.*) Oh no! What happened?

PASTOR. Buddy tried to get Bobo and got stuck with no key.

SISSY. Oh dear! Let me see what I can do. (*She ducks down with searching noises.*) Here it is! I found the key!

BUDDY. You have the keys! How did you get them?

SISSY. Jesus gave them to us—they are keys to the kingdom. The keys to forgiveness.

BUDDY. How will that help? I'm stuck, stuck, stuuuuck!

Sɪssʏ. Shhhh! Shhh! Shhh! It's okay, Buddy. Calm down. We can get you out of there.

Bᴜᴅᴅʏ. How? (*Sobbing.*)

Sɪssʏ. With *forgiveness*—know that God will understand and forgive, and we will too!

Bᴜᴅᴅʏ. I hope so.

Sɪssʏ. Let's try the keys. Pastor, will you help?

(*Together they try the keys and open the chest.*)

Bᴜᴅᴅʏ. Oh, thank you, all of you! I love you!

Sɪssʏ. That's the key! Buddy, you are safe! Oh, I feel like singing!

(*Everyone sings to the melody of the chorus of "Smile a Little Smile for Me, Rosemarie" by the Flying Machine.*)

Sɪssʏ. Share a little prayer with me, and you'll see how we keep on trying.

Bᴜᴅᴅʏ. Add a little faith and see, blest are we!

Thanking God (Luke 17:11–19)

Items needed: three puppets, two broken toys

(*Mikey enters with toy.*)

MIKEY. Buddy? Buddy? Where are you?

BUDDY. Here I am, Mikey. What's up?

MIKEY. Could you fix this for me again?

BUDDY. Sure. Remember how to turn this and wiggle this to fix it?

MIKEY. I do, but you can fix it better than me.

BUDDY. Well okay, but you could learn to fix it yourself.

MIKEY. I know, I know. Thanks! (*Turns to exit.*)

BUDDY. Where are you going? Don't you want to play?

MIKEY. I do. I am going to Ralph's. He has a new train! See you! (*Exits.*)

BUDDY. But, but I'd like to play too. (*Sits and pouts, mumbling.*)

(*Punkin enters.*)

PUNKIN. Pssss… Pspsps… Pspsps…(*Whines.*)

BUDDY. Oh, hi, Punkin. What do you have there?

PUNKIN. Pspsps.

BUDDY. I see. It's just like Mikey's. Oh, and it's broken. Hmmm. Would you like me to fix it?

(*Punkin nods.*)

BUDDY. Sure, no problem. You just have to turn this and wiggle this.

(*Punkin nods, gives Buddy a hug, and turns to leave.*)

BUDDY. Wait! Don't you want to stay and play?

PUNKIN. Psppss, pssssspsssss… Rrrr.

BUDDY. Oh, I see, Ralph has a new train. Go ahead. (*Sits and pouts and mumbles.*)

PASTOR. Buddy, you seem upset.

BUDDY. Well, it seems like my friends only like me when they need something fixed. Hmph!

PASTOR. I see. And I am happy to see that you can help to fix things.

BUDDY. I am happy to fix things, but no one wants to stay and play. (*Whining.*)

PASTOR. That sounds a little like our gospel story for today. Tell me, Buddy, have you remembered to say thank you to God today?

BUDDY. Not today, He didn't do anything today.

PASTOR. Hmmmm. Did you wake up to another day? Did you have a nice breakfast? Were you able to help your friends?

BUDDY. Yes, but—Um… But God didn't—Oh, um—I didn't ask! I guess God did a lot of things for me today, didn't he? Just like I did things for my friends. And I didn't even think about thanking him for all the little things he does all the time.

PASTOR. And I bet God would like someone to just pray and sing and talk with him without having to do anything.

BUDDY. I know he would! Do you think he would like to hear our song?

PASTOR. I bet he would! Let's sing it together. One, two, three…

(*Everyone sings to the melody of the chorus of "Smile a Little Smile for Me, Rosemarie" by the Flying Machine.*)

> Share a little prayer with me, and you'll see
> how we keep on trying.
> Add a little prayer and see, how blest are we!

With, Not in the World (John 17)

Items needed: female puppet, three clear jars—one with water, one with oil, and one empty jar

(*Sissy Bunny enters with one bottle, places it on stage, exits. She returns with a second one, exits, and returns with one empty bottle.*)

SISSY. One water, one oil. Hmmm… Oil and water, I think that will work. It could be a good example…

PASTOR. Good morning, Sissy! What are you planning?

SISSY. I was trying to think of a good example to show Buddy how we can live with the world, but not *in* the world.

PASTOR. Did you see that in today's gospel?

SISSY. I did. Jesus is trying to show us how we can live in this world and stay true to God's Word. It is not easy!

PASTOR. You're right, it's *not* easy. We work and pray with everyone in our world, but have to remember how to be good and kind and loving *all the time*! It is very, very hard.

SISSY. I know! Especially when someone else is not kind or loving to us or someone we love!

PASTOR. Tell me about it!

SISSY. Then while I was making a lunch salad, I got an inspiration! Oil and water!

PASTOR. Oil and water? Oil…and water… Hmm… I don't see it.

SISSY. Maybe we can demonstrate it. Will you help? I only have two paws and no opposable thumbs.

PASTOR. Gladly! Tell me what to do.

SISSY, *gives Pastor the empty bottle.* Please take this.

PASTOR. Okay. (*Shows the empty bottle.*)

SISSY. Now take this water and pour it in. Pretend the water is everyone in our world.

PASTOR, *pours the water and shows the bottle with water.* Okay.

SISSY, *points to the oil.* Now add this. Pretend this is us, trying to be good and kind and loving.

PASTOR, *adds the oil and shows the bottle with water and oil.* Okay, but how?

SISSY. Put the lid on, now shake it up really hard.

PASTOR, *shakes bottle and shows it.* So we get mixed up with everybody in our world when we work together with them…

SISSY. Right! Now hold the bottle still and count to fifteen.

PASTOR, *holds the bottle up high.* One, two, three, four, five… I see something happening. Six, seven… (*He continues counting to fifteen.*)

SISSY. See? When we pause and pray or think about God's Word, we can separate out of our world and find peace in God's world. Just like the oil and water, always separate, God's Word will always help us to be *with* the world while we work, but not *in* the world when we pray.

PASTOR. I see! We can be *with* the world but not *in* the world.

SISSY. I think Buddy may understand that, do you?

PASTOR. I do. And I think I know what you will do next. The song.

SISSY. Of course! Let's all do it together.

(*Everyone sings to the melody of the chorus of "Smile a Little Smile for Me, Rosemarie" by the Flying Machine.*)

> Share a little Faith with me, and you'll see how we keep on trying.
> Add a little prayer and see, blest are we!

Easter People (Doubting Thomas) John 21:24–29

Items needed: puppet, egg

(*Buddy enters with an egg, humming.*)

PASTOR. Good morning, Buddy! What do you have there?

BUDDY. An egg, I brought it to help Thomas.

PASTOR. Thomas? Do we know him?

BUDDY. I think so. He was the one who didn't believe that Jesus had risen.

PASTOR. Do you mean doubting Thomas from today's lesson?

BUDDY. Yes, that's the one! I want to help him understand faith.

PASTOR. Okay, how will you do that?

BUDDY. With this egg.

PASTOR. With an egg? How can you do that with an egg?

BUDDY. Well, you know how God takes care of even the smallest bird?

PASTOR. Yes, go on.

BUDDY. Well, even the smallest bird has great faith.

PASTOR. Is that why the egg is here?

BUDDY. Yes! Just look at that egg. Can you see what is inside?

PASTOR. No, that shell is solid. It protects the baby bird.

BUDDY. That's just it! You or I or even the mama bird cannot see *into* the egg. But she trusts that something amazing is inside. She spends a lot of time sitting on that egg, waiting for it to hatch.

PASTOR. I see. She has faith even though she doesn't see it, and hopes that a baby will hatch. What a good symbol, Buddy! And when the baby hatches, it is a symbol of the new life we celebrate for Easter.

BUDDY. If only Thomas had an egg, then he would not be doubting anymore.

PASTOR. Right you are, Buddy.

BUDDY. If Sissy were here, she would say we are sharing faith and sing her song. How about if we sing it for her?

(*Buddy and Pastor sing to the melody of the chorus of "Smile a Little Smile for Me, Rosemarie" by the Flying Machine.*)

BUDDY AND PASTOR. Share a little faith with me, and you'll see how we keep on trying. Add a little prayer and see, blest are we!

Pentecost (Acts 2:1–21)

Items needed: puppet, birthday balloon

(*Buddy enters and looks around.*)

BUDDY. Ooooh, look at all that red! It's so beautiful! That's my favorite color. What a nice surprise. I can't wait to open all the presents. I just need one more thing.

(Exits after a moment, various noises.)

PASTOR. Buddy, Buddy, are you all right? What are you doing?

BUDDY, *from backstage.* Just getting ready, I have to find one more thing. (*Enters.*) Here it is! I have been saving this for a long time!

PASTOR. What a nice balloon! It says, "Happy Birthday!"

BUDDY. Yes! Happy birthday to me, me, me! (*Sings.*) Happy birthday, it's Buddy's birthday, happy, happy birthday to me!

PASTOR. Oh my, Buddy. Is it really your birthday?

BUDDY. Um, I think so. All the signs are there—decorations in red and candles. I'm even wearing my birthday suit! So where are the presents?

PASTOR. Buddy, it *is* a birthday celebration, but for the church.

BUDDY. What? The church can have a birthday? How does it open presents? That's just silly!

PASTOR. This is the first day that all of Jesus's apostles and disciples received one of the greatest presents ever. The Holy Spirit came and helped them to teach about Jesus.

BUDDY. That sounds scary. Not like a birthday present at all!

PASTOR. Well, it was scary before the Holy Spirit helped them become brave. In fact, they were hiding. And then a great wind came, and the Spirit entered, and they felt braver than ever. So brave that they came out of hiding to tell everyone about God the Father and God the Son and God the Spirit and how much we are loved.

BUDDY. So we are celebrating the birthday of the church. When everyone became brave enough to talk about Jesus and how He came to save us all?

PASTOR. Exactly. And we all get a present—the Holy Spirit to help us become brave too.

BUDDY. That's a pretty awesome present!

PASTOR. It is. Just like the song you taught us about sharing faith. This is a good time to sing it, don't you think?

BUDDY. Yes, All together! One, two, three…

(*Everyone sings to the melody of the chorus of "Smile a Little Smile for Me, Rosemarie" by the Flying Machine.*)

> Share a little faith with me, and you'll see
> how we keep on trying. Add a little prayer and see,
> Blest are we!

About the Author

Anita Louise Brezovic Vance has spent over thirty years working with children of all ages as a teacher, guide, and storyteller. With a bachelor's degree in education and a master's in information science, her studies incorporated best practices for effective learning.

As a lifelong educator, her approach to teaching often included music, roleplaying, and puppetry. During her career, thousands of students became engaged in learning about God's love for us.

This background and these experiences are the basis for a particularly charming and thoughtful puppet play collection.